summersdale

LLAMA-RAMA

EWEN RAMSHORN

LLAMA-RAMA

Summersdale Publishers Ltd
46 West Street
Chichester
West Sussex
PO19 1RP
UK

www.summersdale.com

Printed and bound in Croatia

ISBN: 978-1-78685-349-3

Substantial discounts on bulk quantities of Summersdale books are available to corporations, professional associations and other organisations. For details contact general enquiries: telephone: +44 (0) 1243 771107 or email: enquiries@summersdale.com.

To.....................................

From...................................

Hay,
girl!

Wanna go for a picnic?

ALPACA LUNCH.

You're such a
DRAMA-LLAMA

Llama-glama,

n: a domesticated South
American camelid.

Glama-Llama,

n: a fabulous llama.

Don't be a-llama-ed!

LITERALLY
SHOCKED
AM ONE
SURPRISED
LLAMA
JAW DROP
NO WAY?
SO UNEXPECT

Don't be afraid to

STAND
OUT

from the herd.

Butt's up,
buddy?

HEY BABE, YOU
LOOKING FOR A
**SLICE OF
LLAMA**
WITH THAT DRINK?

I'M FLEECED TO MEET YOU

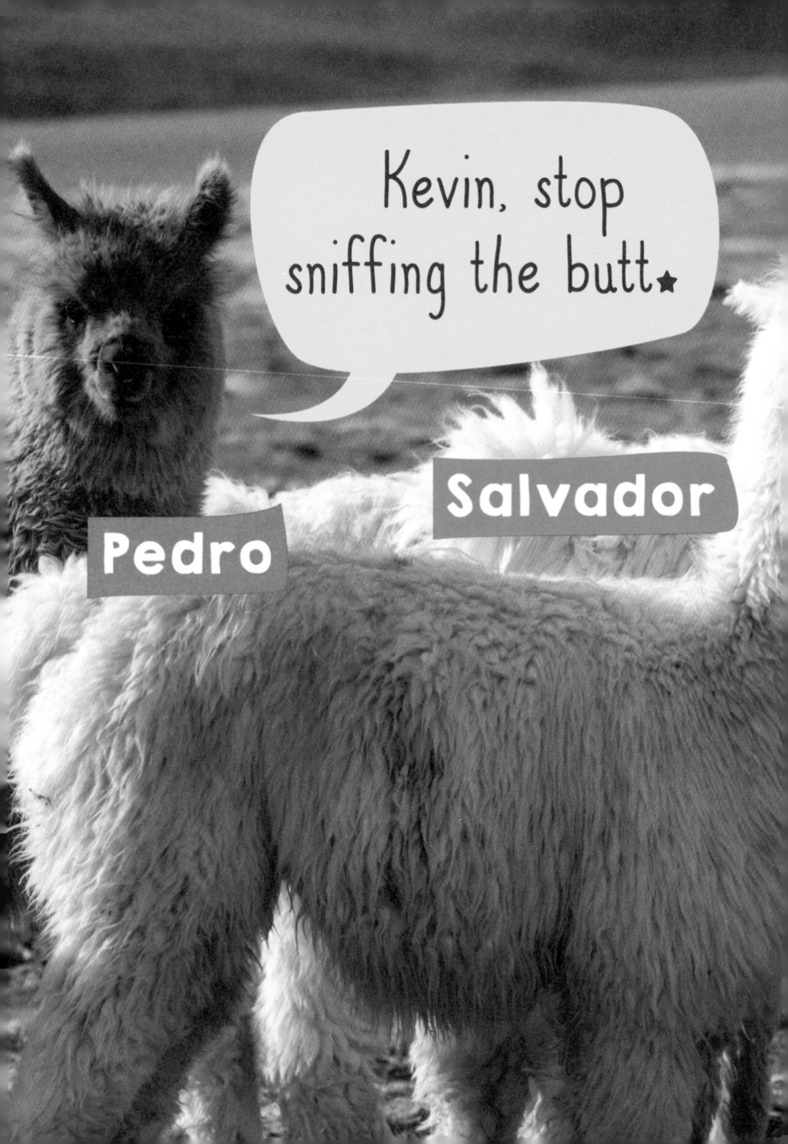
Kevin, stop sniffing the butt★
Salvador
Pedro

Julio

Kevin

This next
song is called
'Peruvian
Vibes'. ⭐

David
Alpacaborough

Mr llover llover

When the
lyrics are
your life.

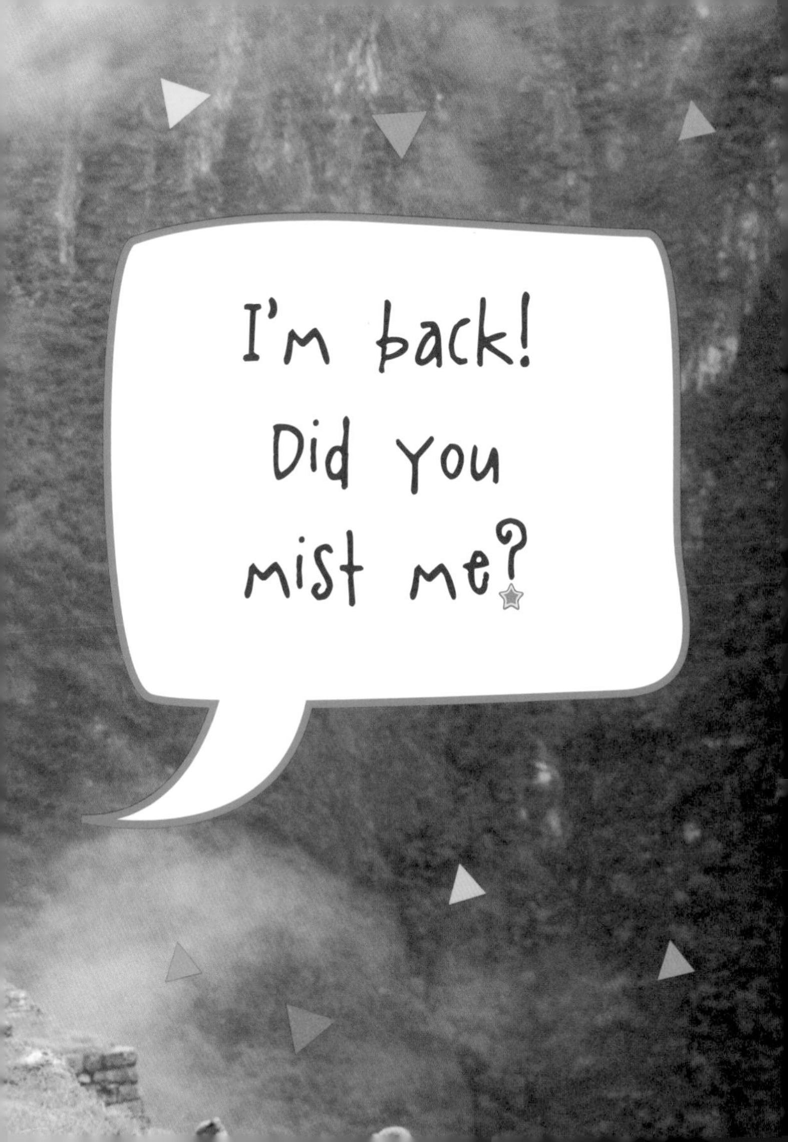
I'm back! Did You mist me?

Big love from
the llam-fam.

PEACE.

They've locked
me up for being a

BAAAD

MAMA-LLAMA.

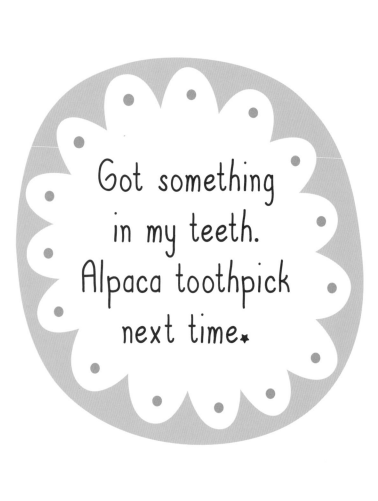

Got something
in my teeth.
Alpaca toothpick
next time.⭐

EEEEEEE
EEEEEEEE
EEEEEEEE
EEEEEEE!

I think I pulled
the wool over
his eyes.

Because you're worth it.

Relationship phase: uploading couples photoshoots to social media.

On the streets
I'm known as

Fierce 'n' Fleecy.

No, my child,
I'm the
Dalai
Llama

IT'S LLAMAGEDDON!

Dude, no
PROB-LLAMA!

The alpacalypse is upon us!

Stop dillying, Margaret, we hoof to be getting on!

When you're
EXTRA
but you
DON'T
CARE.

Have you tried the human filter on your app? Lol!

Don't cry,
little Cria*.

*A cria is a baby llama or alpaca.

You don't
want to see me
when I'm angry.★

Alpaca
punch.★

Good work attaching the GoPro to Ramon's head.

Me and my 'paca trekkin' the tracka.⭐

Costume llama.

Llive ⭐

Llaugh ⭐

Llama ⭐

Image credits:

p.1 – photograph © KarSol/Shutterstock.com
p.1 – hat © BarsRsind/Shutterstock.com
p.1 – stars and cacti © Marish/Shutterstock.com
p.3 – stars © Marish/Shutterstock.com
p.4 – llama © Polina_PM/Shutterstock.com
p.5 © PATRICIA PECEGUINI VIANA/Shutterstock.com
p.6 © fotobook/Shutterstock.com
p.7 – heart © Matisson/Shutterstock.com
pp.7, 9, 11, 12, 13, 15, 19, 20, 23, 24, 26, 28, 31, 36, 40, 43, 44, 46, 47, 48, 51, 52, 56, 59, 60, 63, 64, 67, 68, 70, 71, 72, 73, 75, 76, 79, 80, 82, 84, 87, 88, 91, 92, 93, 96 – star © Marish/Shutterstock.com
p.8 © fotobook/Shutterstock.com
p.9 © Marish/Shutterstock.com
pp.9, 24, 38–39, 84–85 – triangles © Marianne Thompson
p.10 © Abner Veltier/Shutterstock.com
p.11 – crown © notbad/Shutterstock.com
p.11, 82, 83 – bunting © Marianne Thompson
p.12 – triangle icon © LA LA LA/Shutterstock.com
p.12 – flower and leaves icons © Molesko Studio
P.13 – photograph © Jeannette Katzir Photog/Shutterstock.com
P.14 © LOVE_CHOTE/Shutterstock.com
p.15 © Alexey Blogoodf/Shutterstock.com
p.17 © Helen Filatova/Shutterstock.com
p.18 – photograph © Pavel Svoboda Photography/Shutterstock.com
p.19 © Molesko Studio/Shutterstock.com
pp.19, 35 – chillies © Molesko Studio/Shutterstock.com
p.20 – llama © Goosefrol/Shutterstock.com

p.21 © Aline Melo/Shutterstock.com
p.22 © Edijs Volcjoks/Shutterstock.com
p.23 – lime © darsi/Shutterstock.com
p.25 © KarSol/Shutterstock.com
pp.26–27 © Galyna Andrushko/Shutterstock.com
pp.28–29, 36 – guitars © Marish/Shutterstock.com
p.29 – photograph © SimonBarrington/Shutterstock.com
p.30 © Rhys Mitchell/Shutterstock.com
p.31, 71, 93 – sombrero © Marish/Shutterstock.com
p.32 –33 photograph © marktucan/Shutterstock.com
p.32 – cactus © GoodStudio/Shutterstock.com
P.34 – photograph © Lilac Mountain/Shutterstock.com
p.34 – hearts © Molesko Studio/Shutterstock.com
p.35 – heart © Molesko Studio/Shutterstock.com
p.37 – musical notes © Ian O'Hanlon/Shutterstock.com
p.37 – photograph © Fuller Photography/Shutterstock.com
p.38–39 – photograph © Yongyut Kumsri/Shutterstock.com
p.40 – skull © Molesko Studio/Shutterstock.com
p.41 © Pavel Svoboda Photography/Shutterstock.com
P.42 © Andrzej Wilusz/Shutterstock.com
p.43, 59, 79 – chillies – © Marish/Shutterstock.com
p.44 © Molesko Studio/Shutterstock.com
p.45 © Dieter Hawlan/Shutterstock.com
p.46 – photograph © Bildagentur Zoonar GmbH/Shutterstock.com
p.46, 70, 93 – all icons © Marish/Shutterstock.com
p.48 – llama © Good Studio/Shutterstock.com

Every reasonable effort has been made by the publisher to trace and acknowledge the copyright holders of material used in this book. If any errors or omissions are brought to light, the publisher will endeavour to rectify them in any reprints or future editions.

If you're interested in
finding out more about our
books, find us on Facebook at
Summersdale Publishers
and follow us on Twitter at
@Summersdale.

www.summersdale.com